Peter Chidi Okuma

Amazon Synod-German synodal Path: redefining the laity?

Peter Chidi Okuma

Amazon Synod-German synodal Path: redefining the laity?

Fromm Verlag

Imprint
Any brand names and product names mentioned in this book are subject to trademark, brand or patent protection and are trademarks or registered trademarks of their respective holders. The use of brand names, product names, common names, trade names, product descriptions etc. even without a particular marking in this work is in no way to be construed to mean that such names may be regarded as unrestricted in respect of trademark and brand protection legislation and could thus be used by anyone.

Cover image: www.ingimage.com

Publisher:
Fromm Verlag
is a trademark of
International Book Market Service Ltd., member of OmniScriptum Publishing Group
17 Meldrum Street, Beau Bassin 71504, Mauritius

Printed at: see last page
ISBN: 978-613-8-36426-9

Redefining the Laity Today In the light of Today´s Controversy: the *Amazon Synod* vis-à-vis the *German Synodal Path?*

Peter Chidi Okuma

<u>This book is humbly dedicated</u> to:

- **the Divine Mercy via the Blessed Mother of God – the Mother of Priests**

- **To Mum Maria und Pa Franz Dötzer and family**

Table of Contents

Preface

We live in a changing time in human history like many epochs before us. This changing time brings with it new perspectives and new ways of looking at reality and the entire *Weltanschauung* of humanity in the World and in the Church. In spite of the *"sense and insensibilities"*[1] of this epoch, the Gospel of Christ remains very relevant to the men and women of our time – only *application* may differ but the message of Christ *grundsätzlich* remains the same for all times. However, this does not call for nor give room to *compromising* the *key message of Christ* nor that of the *teaching of the Church* – As Christ said: "Heaven *and earth will pass away but my words will not pass away."(Matt 24:35)*The Gospel of Christ does *not adapt* to humanity but humanity adapts herself to the Gospel of Christ. *Self-enclosure* of the Gospel or *kind of Solipsism – of the Gospel* is not meant here. Put another way: Humans and humanity may change but Christ remains eternal – and so are His Words. But in spite of these – *Ecclesia semper reformanda* – the Church of Christ undergoes *Erneuerung* in the hearts of men and women via the influence of the Holy Spirit. And to each human – young and old - men and women – Christians – laity - *all the Baptized in Christ* (Cf, *Lumen Gentium,* Chapter Two – The Church as the people of God) each has a role and *specific ministry* vis-à-vis the calling *(Berufung)* via baptism in the building up of the Body of Christ. There is no confusion here and there should be none. The Gospel of Christ and the Vatican II documents are very succinct on the foregoing.

[1] Cf., Peter Chidi Okuma, *Sense and Insensibilities: Some Urgent Challenges of Postmodernity*, Mauritius, 2019.

Be that as it may, *the lay apostolate is precisely that apostolate which is proper to Laity, which as Christians, they do not sharing in the hierarchical ministry.*[2] In the light of this - it is worth noting here, that article 34 of *Lumen gentium* is in a way a repetition of article 10 to 11; and article 35 in part of article 12. Accordingly, this must have happened when the old chapter on 'the people of God and the Laity' was split into two at the Vatican II Council, and the former sections dealing with the priestly and prophetical aspects of Christian living were carried to Chapter 2.

In sum whether Clergy or laity – we are altogether *Christians* - together we build up the body of Christ - the Church and by extension the world via a *life of witnessing (Testimonium)* – each according specific calling. It is in the light of this that: "*Lumen Gentium* (and *Gaudium et Spes)* must be read in connection with the other conciliar texts, the *Decree on the Apostolate of the Laity* (itself based on the constitution on the Church). They are on the same lines as the Catholic Action inaugurated by Pius XI. This involves no claim to power over society but endeavours to act in society, to undertake that kind of non-violent action which we call influence, the chief instrument of which is bearing witness."

Appreciation

My heartfelt thanks and appreciation go to the Almighty God for His mercies and goodness via the Blessed Mother of God Mary. I am indebted in thanks to His Excellences: Dr. Ludwig Cardinal Müller, Bishop Dr. Gregory Ochiagha (rtd), Bishop Dr. Augustine T. Ukwuoma, and Bishop Dr. Rudolf Voderholzer. My thanks go equally to Dompropst Dr. Franz Frühmorgen, General-vicar Michael Fuchs, Deacon Wolfgang Brandl and the entire *Gremium* of the diocese of Regensburg.

My heartfelt thanks go to my sisters: Lolo Chinyere, Ifeoma, Ifeyinwa, Ebere – my siblings and their families. My gratefulness goes to Lily Uche and family. To Pa Franz and Mum Maria Dötzer and family I remain ever grateful. My thanks goes to my Friend Hon. Sir J.T. U Nnodum (SAN) and Family. And to the members of the Knight of St. Columbus USA - colleagues – I say thanks.

To every single human – young and old who have made positive impact in my life and continue to do so – I remain indebted to you all. I remain grateful to the Catholic Community: Rettenbach and Arrach Bavaria-Germany. I heartfelt appreciation to Fromm Verlag – thanks a million!

Peter Chidi Okuma **2020**

Chapter One

General Introduction

The Amazon synod 2019 was not just about *der Klimawandel und die Kirche...ökologische Bekehrung*[3] (Climate change and the Church – the change in attitude of the Church) – or what the emeritus Pope Benedict XVI designated, as: *"...Schutz der natürlichen Umwelt - eine Frage der Wahrheit und der Liebe"*[4] - but more so about the issue of *redefining the laity and upgrading her mission in the light of the need of the changing times.* The German synod path whose "light-way" was ignited on the first Sunday of Advent 2019 by Reinhardt Cardinal Marx in Munich is purportedly meant to tow the way of the Amazon synod - but more in the light of the crucial and unique need(s) of the German Church vis-à-vis the laity - what could be seen as her new challenging role in the Church in the years and decades ahead.

Be that as it may, the Laity and related issues have been very relevant in every epoch of the Church´s life, but the recent challenges: questions and burning issues of the time before the Church in the postmodern time, today, makes the laity *wider apostolate* in the Church now and in the future much more relevant and challenging in our time as never. There are for example:

---

[3] Cf, Erich Maria Fink and Thomas Maria Rimmel (Editors), *Kirche Heute* – "Amazonas-Synode" Nr., 12. Dezember 2019, pp. 10 – 13.
[4] Cf. Erich Maria Fink and Thomas Maria Rimmel (Editors), *Op. cit.*, pp. 4 – 6. (literal translation in English: *"protection of the natural environment – a question of truth and love."*

• The Amazon Synod of October 2019 and its controversy vis-à-vis the wider mission of the laity in the Church

• There is the controversial German´s Bishops 2020 Conference Synod in alliance with the Laity in the light of the Challenges in the German Church and the wider German society.

• In Sum – these two "burning issues" have been seen as: "the Amazon and Germany: A tale of two synods" - mentioned in the preamble-1 below:

the 06. September 2019 edition of *the Catholic World Report* online edition – the writer Ed Condon reported Pope Francis as saying with the regard to the German Synod:

Francis wrote that the German bishops must avoid seeking to "adapt the Church to the zeitgeist" or proceed with "plans and mechanisms" which could prove "anything but helpful for a common path." Instead, the Pope urged the bishops to focus on evangelization and respect for the *sensus ecclesiae*, which he said "frees us from self-loathing and ideological tendencies."[5]

On the other hand, the same writer reported that the Archbishop of Munich and Freising, Germany Reinhold Cardinal Marx as saying in reply to the Pope´s comment above that:

Marx told reporters in July. "Reading the signs of the times in the light of the Gospel, that's what matters," Marx said.[6]

In the light of the foregoing, these issues seem to reignite the controversial apostolate of the laity in the Church and the controversy

---

[5]https://www.catholicworldreport.com/2019/09/06/analysis-who-are-the-central-committee-of-german-catholics/, consulted on 21/09/2019

[6] Loc. cit.

of/in widening this apostolate in the light of *sensus ecclesiae* of the Church´s mission of *Ecclesia semper Reformanda* vis-à-vis the *Signs of the Times.*

By way of clarity we will try in this work to elucidate the historical critical developments in the ecclesiastical understanding of the Laity. Starting from a more general sketch of the different nuances of the term, we will explore in brief its understanding through the Old Testament, the New Testament, famous theological lexicons, the early church Fathers, some prominent theologians in the modern time; and critically view these historical circumstances preceding the inauguration of Vatican II decree on the Laity - *Apostolicam actuositatem*[7] – in light of the "burning issues" as sampled and reported in divergent views below in: preamble-1, preamble-2, preamble-3 and preamble-4 on these controversial synods: *Amazon* and the *German synodal path.*

Finally, we shall sum up our quest - drawing critical evaluative conclusions vis-à-vis on the controversial synods.

[7] See, "*Apostolicam Actuositatem*, Decree on the Apostolate of the Laity," November 8, 1965, (hereafter cited: A.A.), in *Decretum De Apostolatu Laicorum*, Romae, Typis Polyglottis Vaticanis, 1965. All English translations of this Decree of Vatican II are taken from N. P. TANNER, S.J., (ed.) *Decrees of the Ecumenical Councils, Vol. II (Trent to Vatican II),* London, 1990."

Chapter Two

The Thesis Statements

2.1 Preamble - 1

The Amazon and Germany: A tale of two synods

By JD Flynn

September 16, 2019 The Catholic World Report[8] - Catholic News Agency

For the next two months, most of the ink spilled by Catholic journalists will be dedicated to the Amazon, and especially the three-week Rome meeting of bishops in October that will discuss the region. But while the Amazon synod of bishops holds popular attention, some astute Church-watchers will be more attentive to the emerging controversy surrounding a different synod, to be held in Germany.

The pan-Amazonian synod has become the latest battleground in the long series of internecine conflicts that have plagued the Church in recent years. Conservative figures have decried the synod's preparatory documents as pantheistic heterodoxy, while progressive Churchmen have cast the meeting as the occasion of some kind of new beginning for the Church, after which, at least one bishop has said, "nothing will be the same."

At issue, at least theoretically, are two loaded topics in the Church's life: the possibility of ordaining married men to the priesthood, and

[8] *The Catholic World Report*, Consulted on 21/09/2019

the quagmire surrounding questions of "inculturation," which ask how the Gospel can be expressed in diverse cultural settings.

The topic of ordaining married men is on the table because the remoteness of some Amazon villages, which almost never see a priest, has led to the suggestion that ordained "*viri probati*," older, married men, could make it possible for more Catholics to have access to the sacramental life.

But there is concern among some that considering the possibility of married priests in the Amazon region, where priests are few, will lead to widespread adoption of the practice, and the loss of the custom of clerical celibacy. There is also concern that a broadly applied dispensation from the obligation of priestly celibacy will stir-up the simmering debate over ordaining women to the diaconate, and even the officially settled argument over ordaining women as priests.

While most proponents of the possibility say their sights are fixed only on the problems of Amazonia, critics are skeptical. Among advocacy groups, intellectuals, and even a few bishops, heated rhetoric has begun to fly.

As the synod grows closer, the rhetoric will grow only more intense, from all corners of the Church.

Rome will host an entire cottage industry of pundits in the weeks preceding the synod, and "experts," from both the left and the right, will hold symposia and conferences, trying to make the case that the synod matters, that their opponents are wrong and that, whatever their viewpoint, it is the only legitimately Catholic perspective on the matters at hand.

The pan-Amazonian synod, in short, is likely to follow the playbook that has characterized the two most recent synods in Rome, beginning with the 2015 Synod on the Family. After that meeting, which is best remembered for a fracas over divorce and communion, a 2018 synod on youth and young people was similarly polemical.

The conflicts surrounding synods are unfortunate, for at least two reasons. In the first place, they distract from the sincere and earnest conversation that might take place among bishops about critical issues.

Synods are supposed to be conversations, and the topics discussed are usually ones about which many people in Church leadership or pastoral ministry have something to contribute, or something to learn. The Amazon region, in which Pentecostalism is overtaking Catholicism, in which child labor and human trafficking are serious issues, and deforestation threatens whole communities, is in need of the Church's leadership and pastoral presence. A conversation, rather than a debate, over the issues in the Amazon would be of real benefit to the Church there. But conflict over hot-button issues, and a sense that the synod is a gladiatorial contest between warring sides, is likely to blunt that conversation.

Conflict over synods of bishops is unfortunate mostly because there is very little to be gained from it. Synod assemblies are low-stakes affairs: synods have no power, they cannot make policies or declare doctrine or do anything, except publish documents to be reviewed by the pope as he formulates his thoughts on the topic under discussion. Synods are consultative conversations. They do not bind the pope, or instruct him. They just offer the advice of a usually diverse-thinking assembly of leaders.

Synods have grown contentious because Pope Francis used his 2016 post-synodal document *Amoris laetitia* to signal an openness to the possibility that divorced and remarried people could, under certain circumstances, receive the Eucharist while remaining in a sexual relationship. That suggestion has been extremely divisive, and because it is associated with the family synod of 2015, at least some bishops have begun to treat synods as though they are convened to legislate for the Church. They are not convened for that purpose.

And the pope could have introduced his ideas about divorce, remarriage, and the Eucharist in any way he chose. He happened to do it in a post-synodal document, but not because the synod in some way freed him to do so, or mandated that he do so. It is sometimes suggested that the synod gave him some political cover, but since the idea did not have full-throated support from the synod's participants, the hypothesis seems flimsy.

In short, nothing about the synod compelled, authorized, or permitted the pope to teach as he did. But because of *Amoris laetitia*, and the controversial synod of 2015, pundits seem now to characterize each synod not as an exchange of ideas, but as a battle for the pope's endorsement.

While the stakes of the pan-Amazonian synod are far lower than they're usually perceived, the stakes of a showdown over a synod in German are much higher than has likely been realized by many Catholics.

The German bishops are planning a two-year "synodal pathway" in the country. The idea is to bring bishops together with lay people, especially those associated with the Central Committee of German Catholics, to pass "binding resolutions," on controversial topics, including sexual morality and clerical leadership.

The planned synod in Germany is not intended to be a conversation. It is intended to redefine the course of Christianity in Germany, even while giving new consideration to long-established points of Christian doctrine.

The Vatican has warned the German bishops not to continue with their plans, noting that a synod of the type planned by the Germans would disrupt the Church's life, and could cause a catastrophe by denying the Church's doctrinal teaching.

But the German bishops, under the leadership of Cardinal Reinhard Marx, have insisted that the synod will proceed, and that the Vatican simply doesn't understand what's at stake.

Marx will meet with Vatican officials this week. The cardinal hopes to persuade the Vatican to allow him to proceed with his plans. He is not in a position to back down, because he has assured the Central Committee of German Catholics, which includes advocates of same-sex marriage, that they will have a deliberative voice in the future of the German Church. Relenting, for Marx, would likely mean losing his support among secular German figures, and, by admitting that the Vatican was right, falling out of favor among the Churchmen who support him.

Cardinal Marx, by some estimates, seems to be playing a kind of ecclesiastical game of chicken with the Vatican, and batting that the pope's Curia will back down before he does.

But if the Vatican does not relent, and the Germans push forward, a great deal is at stake: some experts have suggested that if the Germans proceed with their synodal path in defiance of instructions from Pope Francis and the Vatican, they run the risk of being declared in schism.

At the moment, Marx seems unintimidated by efforts from two different Vatican offices to rein in Germany's planned synodal process. He might be persuaded, if at all, only by a direct and personal intervention from Pope Francis.

Marx is said to be persuasive with Pope Francis, but sources tell CNA that the pope is growing impatient with the cardinal's approach to the German synod. If Francis has to intervene, and Marx does not accept the pope's direction, the result would be a serious crisis for the Church in Germany. The situation is still developing.

The pan-Amazonian synod will provide plenty of fodder for debate this autumn. But a serious ecclesiological crisis is unfolding in Germany, and how it will be resolved remains to be seen.

2.2 Preamble - 2

UNDERSTANDING THE DEBATE OVER MARRIED PRIESTS AT THE AMAZON SYNOD[9]

• John L. Allen Jr. EDITOR – *CRUX* - Jun 18, 2019

Every so often, we get official confirmation of the obvious, and, surprisingly enough, it still makes waves. Such is the case again this week with the release of a preparatory document for an October summit of bishops on the Amazon, which confirms that the ordination of married "elderly people," meaning men, will be on the agenda.

From the moment the Synod of Bishops on the Amazon was announced, it's been clear that the issue of the *viri probati*, meaning *tested married men* who are pillars of their communities, would come up. Requests for consideration of the possibility have been voiced with increasing urgency by bishops and other Catholic personnel from the region for decades, and it was basically unthinkable a whole synod would go by without it being floated again. Crux spoke to a Brazilian theologian in February who said then that the *viri probati* would be discussed when the bishops meet.

Nonetheless, given all the lengths to which Rome has gone over the years to squash consideration of married priests, seeing the topic on an official Vatican agenda is still a bit arresting.

To understand the nature of the discussion we're likely to see in October, here are three essential things to understand.

---

[9] *CRUX*, consulted on:21/09/2019.

First, the debate is not over whether the Catholic Church can have married priests. It already does, and plenty of them. The 23 Eastern churches in communion with Rome have married priests, and in the United States, there are hundreds of former Episcopalians, Methodists, Lutherans and others who were married in their original denominations and permitted to remain married as Catholic priests (Italics mine).

The question, therefore, is not whether to have married priests, but whether to have more of them (Italics mine).

As a corollary, no one is talking about eliminating celibacy for the vast majority of priests in the Latin Rite.

Second, this discussion will be very different from debate over married priests in the U.S. or Western Europe, because it's basically not ideological.

In the West, more liberal Catholics sometimes press for a married clergy on grounds that celibacy is unnatural and breeds sexual dysfunction, often linking it to the clerical sexual abuse crisis. Such activists also sometimes make the argument that by creating a special caste of unmarried men, celibacy contributes to clericalism, elitism, a detachment from the struggles of ordinary families, and all manners of other ills.

Whatever one makes of the merits of those arguments, they're not what drives discussion of the *viri probati* in the Amazon, or for that matter in most other parts of the world.

Americans often complain of a priest shortage, but the statistical fact of the matter is that the U.S. is priest-rich compared to everywhere other than Western Europe. In the U.S. there's one priest for every 1,300 baptized Catholics. Across Latin America it's 1 to 7,000, in sub-Saharan Africa it's 1 to 5,300, and in the Caribbean it's 1 to 8,300.

In some Latin American nations, including several that share the Amazon, those ratios in some dioceses can soar as high as 1 to 16,000 or 17,000. Moreover, the isolation of many rural communities in the Amazon, which are accessible only by boat or by horseback up steep mountain climbs, sometimes means they see a priest only once every few weeks, perhaps once every six months or so.

Routine sacramental life under such circumstances is obviously impossible. Mass, confession, and so on, which are the backbone of Catholic life most places, is exceedingly rare, and those communities feel the absence of it. It's almost like being under a sort of geographical interdict, except for the fact these people have committed no sin to warrant it.

For bishops from these parts of the world, the issue of the *viri probati* isn't a question of left v. right, and some of the prelates campaigning for it are otherwise among the deepest theological and political conservatives you'll ever meet. It's also not tied to any larger diagnosis of what's ailing the Church – it's instead a simple practical matter of wanting to be able to provide the sacraments to their people on a regular basis.

As a further benefit, the *viri probati* would also be a way of empowering indigenous communities and ministering to them from within, since the candidates would come from those communities themselves.

Third, this fall's debate will be just that – a debate. It's not a foregone conclusion that the *viri probati* will enjoy majority support, and although a synod is merely advisory and Pope Francis can do whatever he wants, he will certainly be listening.

I've been covering synods of bishops for more than 20 years, and I honestly can't remember very many in which the *viri probati* didn't come up – never on the formal agenda before, but always in the air.

At the 2005 Synod on the Eucharist, for example, several bishops from the global south mentioned areas in the developing world, including Latin America and the Pacific Islands, where isolated communities strung out over vast distances often go without priests for long periods of time. Bishop Roberto Camilleri Azzopardo of Comayaga, Honduras, reported having one priest for every 16,000 Catholics in his diocese. Several bishops suggested that the Church might consider the ordination of *viri probati*.

That effort was turned back by other bishops, mostly from the global north, determined to defend the spiritual and pastoral value of priestly celibacy. In the end, the synod issued a reaffirmation of celibacy. Granted, there won't be many northern bishops at this synod, but those views still will be heard.

That's especially likely to be the case given the global village dynamic of Catholicism these days. Even if permission for the *viri probati* were to be granted only for a highly circumscribed geographical location, it would set a precedent, and it wouldn't take long for activists elsewhere to begin seeking the same latitude.

While it’s anyone’s guess what might happen during the Oct. 6-27 synod, one thing is for sure: By putting married priests on the agenda, the Vatican has ensured that a much wider audience will be tuning in.

2.3 Preamble – 3

The upcoming controversial German-Bishops synodal path and its implications!

September 30, 2019 (LifeSiteNews) – Father Gero P. Weishaupt, a German priest with a doctorate in canon law, just wrote a commentary in light of the recent fall assembly of the German bishops. At this assembly, they decided to start a "synodal path" questioning the Church's teaching on celibacy, the all-male priesthood, and homosexuality, among others.

Two German prelates – Cardinal Rainer Woelki and Bishop Rudolf Voderholzer – strongly oppose this controversial choice of topics for the "synodal path," and Voderholzer announced already that he might at some point leave this event.

Dr. Weishaupt entitled his own commentary on the problem of the "synodal path" To Take Seriously the Penal Law, which already indicates the theme of his text.

Weishaupt received his doctorate from the Gregoriana in Rome and since then has served as judge at diocesan tribunals, as a curial secretary in Rome, as a Latin expert for Radio Vatikan (the German section of Vatican Radio), as a professor at the Benedict XVI University Heiligenkreuz (Austria), and as the editor of the Catholic website Kathnews.

Right at the beginning of his article, Weishaupt makes it clear that the discussion about the possibility of "ordaining" female "priests" is a "questioning of a definitive, infallible and unchangeable doctrine of the Church." The "unending" discussion in Germany on this matter is therefore "a criminal offense."

"The Apostolic See would now have to admonish the majority of the German Bishops' Conference and the members of the Central Committee of German Catholics [ZdK, a lay organization that takes a leading role in the 'synodal path'] and, should there be no revocation, then to sanction them with a penalty."

Weishaupt makes it clear that, "he who wishes to discuss a topic, puts the object of the discussion into question, otherwise, a discussion would be superfluous."

After some detailed explanations of a 1998 document by Pope John Paul II as to the nature of different infallible doctrines (those that are part of the deposit of the faith as revealed by God and those which are infallible without the Church saying that they "have been revealed by God"), Dr. Weishaupt explains that Pope John Paul II, for the "protection of these definitive doctrines of the faith which are most intimately connected with the revealed deposit of the faith, in a historical and logical manner," had also established penal norms.

Those Catholics who reject a doctrine and don't recant that rejection should be punished. (can. 1371 § 1) Accordingly, can. 750 § 2 explains that everything has to be held "that has been presented by the Magisterium of the Church concerning faith and morals as being definitive." He who rejects these teachings finds himself in "resistance to the teaching of the Catholic Church."

Dr. Weishaupt then presents to his readers Pope John Paul II's 1994 document *Ordinatio Sacerdotalis*, in which the Pope writes, "I declare that the Church has no authority whatsoever to confer priestly ordination on women and that this judgment is to be definitively held by all the Church's faithful."

Since the German bishops and some members of the ZdK have already declared that they wish to discuss the matter of female "priests," Weishaupt continues, this decision is "an act of disobedience toward the Pope and the Church's Magisterium," to include a "rejection of an infallible, definite doctrine.

"Therefore," he explains, "the criminal offense according to can. 1371 § 1 is fulfilled."

"It would now be the duty of the Apostolic See first to admonish those bishops of the German Bishops' Conference who wish to discuss this doctrine, as well as the members of the Zdk, according to the precepts of can. 1371 § 1," Weishaupt states.

"If, on the part of the majority of the German bishops and of the ZdK, there does not follow a recantation," the canon lawyer continues, "there should be imposed upon them a 'just penalty,' which does not exclude the excommunication of the concerned bishops and of the members of the ZdK, as well as, in reference to bishops, the removal from the episcopal office as the highest form and ultima ratio of ecclesial penalties."

Weishaupt explains that, since the outbreak of the sex abuse crisis in the Church, the Church's penal law has been "rediscovered," "after it had been gravely neglected in the wake of the Second Vatican Council."

“The abuse crisis,” the canon law expert continues, “led to a deepened insight that penalties are necessary.”

He also draws a connection to the German “synodal path” and its questioning of dogmatic teachings of the Catholic Church, saying that such questioning also “damages the Church.”

“It will be seen,” Dr. Weishaupt concludes, “whether the Church will apply in a resolute manner the penal law with regard to the ‘synodal’ discussion of the definitively settled doctrine that the priestly ordination can only be conferred on men.”

2.4 Preamble - 4

Lay Catholic leaders warn about Amazon Synod: 'Pope Francis has gravely harmed the faith. It is time to say it out loud.'

ROME, October 4, 2019 (LifeSiteNews) — Lay Catholic leaders from around the world, increasingly alarmed about the upcoming Amazonian Synod and how it threatens to disfigure and "Protestantize" the Church, gathered not far from the Vatican today to discuss their grave concerns.

The roundtable discussion, titled "Our Church – reformed or deformed?" was hosted by the international pro-life association Voice of the Family. Over 5,000 people across the continents tuned in.

On the eve of the synod, they described the multifaceted diabolical menace to the Catholic Church it portends to be. Their choice of strong language reflects the peril they sense: That after the synod, what will emerge will no longer be the Catholic Church.

"We have arrived. This week the Amazonian Synod will be underway," said John-Henry Westen, co-founder and editor-in-chief of LifeSiteNews. "It is expected to be the most severe calamity for the faith the Church has ever known and let's pray that it won't turn out as dire as it threatens."

“A few cardinals have warned of apostasy and heresy in the working document prepared for the Synod, but most have remained silent,” continued Westen. “We, the faithful, cannot remain silent because it is the faith of our children that is being threatened. It is our right as Catholics to have the faith of Jesus Christ handed down faithfully by our priests and bishops and especially the Pope.”

“There are, at this moment, two religions within the Catholic Church,” declared Professor Roberto de Mattei.

“The first is the traditional Catholicism, the religion of those who, in the current confusion, continue to be faithful to the immutable Magisterium of the Church,” said de Mattei.

“The second, until a few months ago without a name, now has a name: it is the Amazonian religion because, as declared by the person currently governing the Church, there is a plan to give the Church ‘an Amazonian face,’” explained de Mattei.

“Two religions cannot coexist within the same Church,” he reaffirmed.

“At the Pan-Amazon Synod, will we see the Church abandon that Divine Commission to convert and baptize all nations?” wondered Michael Matt, publisher of The Remnant, who spoke about the disappearance of traditional missionaries and religious orders.

He asked: “Will the Vatican bless and approve a certain indigenous theology whose animating principle is essentially pagan? Will the Church teach that pagan cultures themselves are of God because to suggest otherwise would be to engage in a sort of religious supremacism that holds Christianity as the only true religion?”

“Now we face a synod of bishops that promises to embrace an indigenous theology that would essentially abandon the Church’s missionary effort altogether while embracing an eco-theology that would send forth missionaries of climate change to teach all nations to listen to the cry of Mother Earth,” declared Matt.

“Please God, may this not come to pass, for if it does it will surely represent the Catholic Church’s formal surrender to the world and to the spirit not just of the age but also the jungle,” he pleaded.

José Antonio Ureta, a leader of the international Tradition, Family, and Property (TFP) movement in France, warned that if the synod fathers and Pope Francis approve the measure in the *Instrumentum laboris* (working document) to ordain elderly married men as priests, “neo-Lutheranism will have defeated the Council of Trent.”

“But, alas! Such new ecclesiastic structure based on a non-ministerial and non-hierarchical priesthood will no longer be the Catholic Church,” said Ureta.

“Pope Francis and his clerical allies are creating a globalist organization with a Catholic-appearing face,” said Church Militant’s Michael Voris. “What is emerging is not Catholic. The façade should be dropped and for once truth be allowed to prevail.”

Voris explained that Pope Francis has moved the Church to “align with a counterfeit kind of theology inspired by godless atheism, and in the rush to advance this, he’s surrounded himself with numerous clerical scoundrels — some who have been complicit in the performing of or cover-up of sex abuse of minors or young adults, mostly male."

"The Catholic Church has been infiltrated from within and this infiltration goes back at least to the pontificate of Pope Pius IX," said Catholic author Dr. Taylor Marshall. "It is an attack on the supernatural faith, miracles, divine revelation, and upon the origin of our creation: God's identity of male and female, the institution of human matrimony, and the natural law precept to be fruitful and multiply with marriage. Moreover, it is a resurrection of paganism 'that you might become gods.'"

"Pope Francis has signed a document in Abu Dhabi which contains a sentence which has explosive consequences for the Catholic faith," said Italy's Marco Tosatti. "Here it is: 'The pluralism and diversity of religions, colour, gender, race and language are willed by God in His wisdom.' The implications of a sentence of this kind are evident: if God has willed … that several religions should exist, it can be inferred that all religions are the divine will and therefore any person is free to choose the religion most suited to him or her."

"This sentence is profoundly wrong from a Christian – and Catholic – standpoint," said Tosatti.

"Personally, I believe that this declaration is one of the most devastating sentences for Catholicism ever uttered by a Pope, and that it is a substantial affirmation of relativism," he added.

"Among the most obviously threatening innovations that are being introduced by the upcoming Amazon Synod is the promotion of some form of ordained ministry for women," asserted French journalist Jeanne Smits.

She warned that the Indian theology which the synod will promote demands the ordination of women as ministers. "It is within the logic of traditional indigenous spirituality, that is, paganism. Or if you want to take it a bit further: idolatry."

"The Amazon Synod will be arguing about the role of women in the Church, when the Church already has the most beautiful answer to that argument: the Virgin Mary," declared Smits. "When God made the Cosmos – which means beauty – He was making a fitting earthly home and dowry for His Daughter, Mother, and Bride. She is our Queen, the Queen of the universe and even the Queen of the Angels, much to Satan's discontent, since he must submit to and be conquered by a mere woman, by a mother who can communicate to us eternal life through the sacrifice of her Beloved Son."

"Our vision of woman is defined by that. What more could we possibly want?" asked Smits.

Accusation, fervent intercession, and a 'time for heroes and saints'

"With all respect owed to the ecclesiastical authorities, I accuse all those who have approved, or will approve, the *Instrumentum laboris* on the Amazon, of polytheism and, more specifically, *polydemonism* because, quoting Psalm 95, 'All divinities of the Gentiles are Demons; our Lord has instead created the heavens,'" said de Mattei.

"I call upon the cardinals and bishops who are still Catholic to raise their voices against this scandal. If their silence continues, we will continue to seek the intervention of the Angels and Mary Queen of

Angels, to save the Holy Church from every form of reinvention, distortion, and reinterpretation," added de Mattei.

John-Henry Westen pointed out that despite all the grave concerns raised by the panelists, This "is not to say that we don't love Pope Francis. Indeed, it would not be love at all to gloss over these monumental concerns and be silent about them, because they harm him most of all. He will have to answer to Christ at judgement just like we all will."

"We must continue to pray for the Pope every day, pray for his conversion," said Westen.

"It doesn't take a theologian to recognize when the faith is being distorted," he added. "We won't leave the Church; it is the One True Church and there is no other. We shall fight for Christ's truth in the Church because we are ready to die for this faith."

During the question and answer period, when the inevitable question about the possibility of schism was raised, Professor de Mattei said we must pray for "a real counter-reformation, a counter-revolution, a restoration of the real Christianity."

Though we are waging war against the forces of chaos in the Church, "The division of our enemy is our strength," said de Mattei.

"This is a scary moment," said Michael Matt. "If this synod goes as predicted by several cardinals, this is the biggest news story in the history of the world with the exception of the crucifixion of God. Nothing is bigger than the Bride of Christ raising, hoisting the flag of surrender."

"If this happens, this is a huge story and great people are going to come to the defense of the Church – heroes and saints," proclaimed Matt. "Let's prepare our children for a crusade, and let's inspire them."

Chapter Three

3.1 *Laity-nuancing* in light of the *Controversial synods*

In light of the foregoing how do we *nuance* the notion of the "laity" when *"viri probati" – older, trusted and tested married men* - "laity" suddenly graduate to the next level to become "ordained priest?" And perhaps women suddenly become Deaconess? Does that mean really a *paradigm shift* in the understanding and grasp of the notion of the laity? How can historical-critical study assist us in this controversy and impending mindset?

It is a critical fact that most eminent theologians who had ventured into study on the Laity and her related apostolate had only done this through traditional insights. And this is not enough to tackle the challenging times; instead, this writer thinks that: "there is a need for a critical vis-a- vis a historical study of the dominant theories about the *layperson* in light of today´s critical challenges as seen in the light of the two controversial synods mentioned above *in the thesis statements.*

Be that as it many, critical-historical studies have shown that the word *laicus,* which is at the root of the word *laity,* means originally something *profane, which* excludes the notion of "sacred".[10] The sense in which the Greek word λάος*[11]* from which λάίκος, is derived, has not the general meaning of *populus,* but rather its restrictive sense as part of the people.[12]

---

[10] J. DE LA POTTERIE, SJ. ' L'origine et le sens primitif du mot laic' in *Nouvelle Revue Théologique (hence* NRT) 80, 1958, p.852. See also, CONGAR, Y. M-J, *Jalons pour une théologie du laïcat,* (*Unam Sanctam 23)*, Paris, 1953, p.19; the entire *Chapitre Premier* is devoted to resolving this semantics of meaning.
[11] A keen reading of Justin, *Dial.* 123,
[12] J. de la Potterie, *Loc. cit.*

Erudite scholar like Potterie demonstrates that, that word, 'laikos' does not derive as was commonly assumed, from the Greek λαός in the sense of "the mass of the people." It refers, rather, to the distinction within God's people of the consecrated members from those who are not consecrated, between the priest and those, "who are not qualified."

Gregory Dix (OSB) argues, that λάος signifies a member of God's people in the East about the year 300A.D; by about 450A.D. it has almost come to mean something *'profane'* as opposed to the 'sacred.' This would be associated with those ideas, which, in public worship, ended in the separation of the celebrant from the congregation (rood screen, *έικοΰοσταοϊς*). Among other terms used in the East to signify lay people were ιδιωτά*i (Chrysostom),* corresponding to the laicus=ιδίώτά=illiterate of the Middle Ages; and βίώτικοϊ *(ΰομόκάνών),* corresponding to the Latin *saeculares.*[13] In sum, Dix shows that, *laos* is equated to the people of the New Covenant.

F. Wulf and J. B. Bauer have also shown convincingly that, though λάίκος comes from λάος philologically, its historical, pre-Vatican II semantic significance is not and should not be connected with λάος in the sense of the people of God. According to these duos the meaning of the term is to be understood from the perspective that distinguishes the λάίκος, from the priest and Levite.[14]

---

[13] Cf. G. DIX, in *The Shape of the Liturgy*, London, 1945, p.480.Also, In the book, *The Apostolic Ministry,* London, 1946, p.285.

[14]F. WULF, "Ueber die Herkunft und den Ursprunglichen Sinn des Von 'laicus'," in *Geist und Leben*, 32, 1959, pp.62-63. See also, J. B. BAUER, "Die Wortgeschichte Von 'laicus'," in *Zeitscrift fur katholische Theologie,* 81, 1959, pp.224-228. The duos have in these articles taken pains to explicate the intricacies of the semantics and use of this concept.

The *Kirchenlexicon* of Wetzer and Welte (1891), dismisses the word 'Layman' (Laity) with a simple reference to 'clergy.'[15] One wonders loudly on the reason behind this outstanding negligence. Is it to downplay the role of the 'common man and woman' as against that of the Clergy - the hierarchy in the Church or is it a mere oversight by the composers and arrangers of the Lexicon? Could this oversight have come from instructions from the high quarters? Or is it backed-up by the strict fact of the hegemony then, of the German hierarchy?

The *Dictionnaire de théologie catholique* (1967) defines the 'Laity' in terms of 'membership of the Church of Christ'.[16] Later ecclesiological lexicons like, *Handbuch theologischer Grundbegriffe* (1963) did not make the omission that *Kirchenlexicon* did years earlier. Instead, it sees the term, 'Laity' as purely of a religious suggestion.[17] Whereas, *Lexikon für Theologie und Kirche* (1997) conceives the meaning of the term, 'laity' in terms of the 'commitment to the people',[18] while tracing its *historisch-theologische* origin to St Clement,[19] the text in

[15] See, WETZER & WELTE, *Kirchenlexicon* VII, Fribourg, Brisgau, 1891(col. 1323: *Laien*, s. *Clerus*).?

[16] B. LOTH et A. MICHEL, *Dictionnaire de théologie catholique*, deuxième partie, Paris, 1967, p.2862. "Du fait de son appartenance à l'église, et, par elle et en elle, au Christ, le laïc à une vocation à l'apostolat. Sans doute, l'église, institution du Christ, comporte nécessairement une hiérarchie." See also, P. Van Der MEER, F. BAUR, & L. ENGELBRET, *De Katholieke Encyclopaedie,* Zestiende deel, Amsterdam, Antwerpen,1953, p.321. "Leek(Lat. Laicus, „tot het volk behorend", Greek. Laos = volk), sedert de vroegste tijdens benaming voor een gelovige, in het meervoud voor het gehele Christelijke volk tengenover geestelijke en geestelijkheid, de dragers der kerkelijke macht."

[17] H. FRIES, (ed.), *Handbuch Theologischer Grundbegriffe,* Band II (Laie bis Zeugnis), München, 1963,pp.14-15. "Der Begriff Laie ist ein christlicher Begriff. Seine heidneischen Vorgänger, die die (sic) sprachgeschichtliche Forschung zutage förderte, beinhalten nur eine partielle Analogie soziologischer Ordnung. Der Begriff hat seinen vollen positiven Sinn nur in der Kirche, sofern diese eine originale Realität ist, eine Abschnitt im Gesamtgefüge einer Ekkesiologie sein mit den allgemeinstein, noch ganz unentfalteten, aber inhaltschweren, alles einzelne zusammenfassenden Aussagen über das Mysterium der Kirche. Am Anfang dieses Versuches, Statut und Rolle der Laien festzulegen, muss man sich Statut und Rolle der Kirche selbst in Erinnerung rufen."

[18] W. KASPER, et. al. *Lexikon für Theologie und Kirche*, (Sechster band), Freiburg, Basel, Rom, Wien, 1997.p.587. "Laie ist vergleich λαός abgeleitet und bedeutet, dem Volk zugehörig." "

[19] *Loc. cit.* "Der Begriff λαικός kommt christlich erstmal in 1Clem. 40,5."

the light of *kirchenrechtlich* conceives the 'Laity' as 'believers,' 'Christ faithful people,' those baptized in Christ.`[20]

In the Code of Canon Law, one discovers that in the old text of 1917, out of a total of 2,414 canons, one finds only 44 canons in the chapter 'De Laicis'. Most of the time, '*laicus*' signifies every faithful who is not a cleric. For example, Canon 107(old canon) reads: "By divine institution there are in the Church clerics distinct from the laity...."[21] This distinction and opposition are certainly a basic concept of *laicus* in the Code of 1917. The reason behind this distinction, which determines the clerical and lay states (the Laity) here are the divine and the hierarchical structure of the Church and its hierarchical offices.[22]

Furthermore, in the new Code of Canon of 1983, concerning the 'laity,' one observes that it follows closely the development in the Dogmatic Constitution on the Church, *Lumen Gentium* by titling the Book II of the Code, 'the Christian Faithful' (*De Christifidelibus*). The 'Christian faithful' (laity?) are defined as, "those who, as they have been incorporated in Christ through baptism, have been constituted as the people of God...."[23]; Book II, title II and title III make distinction between 'Lay Christian Faithful' (*Christifideles laici*) and Sacred Ministers or Clerics (De *ministris sacris seu de Clericis*).

---

[20] *Ibid.* p.594. "Laie nur sind Gläubige (, christifideles"), die durch die - Taufe Christus eingegliefachen – Amt Christi teilhaft geworden sind."

[21] Canon. 107, par. I, in *Codex Iuris Canonici*, Romae, 1918; "Ex divina institutione sunt in Ecclesia *clerici* a *laicis* distincti...." Italics are mine. See also, Canon 120 par.2 here, *laicus* has to be interpreted as *civilis*, which is opposite to *ecclesiasticus*.

[22] "Dogmatic Constitution on the Church, *Lumen. Gentium"* Nov.21, 1964, [hereafter cited, *Lumen Gentium* and abbreviated as *L. G.*] In *Acta Apostolicae Sedis*, (hence, AAS) 57(1965*)*, nn. 13,18; see also, L. G. nn. 43, 74.

[23] Can. 204, par. I, in *Codex Iuris Canonici*, Liberia Editrice Vaticana, Typis Polyglottis Vaticanis, 1983; "Christifideles sunt qui, utpote per baptismum Christo incorporati, in populum Dei sunt constituti...."

Departing from the above - Yves Marie-Joseph Congar attempts a more exact descriptive nuancing[24] of the Laity which is 'theological and not merely sociological,'[25] with the following formula: (a) Laymen do not live exclusively for the realities of heaven; this is the condition of monks in so far as this life allows it; (b) While the Laity are Christians in the full sense of the word, living a life in Christ, still they do not have competence, or at least their competence is limited, over the means to this life in Christ which are properly ecclesiastical, means which are within the competence of clerics.[26]

In his prominent book on the laity, 'the Laity' emerge above all else, as members of the People of God, that is to say, Christians. At the same time, he refers to the three modalities of being Christians: sacred ministers, laity, and religious. This distinction is in accord with a terminology that goes back to the third century, reflecting a "permanent" structure in the Church. It is with these terms that Congar formally proposes his theology of the laity[27] within the framework of a renewed ecclesiology.[28]

Karl Rahner defines the *Laity* in their relations to the World. This is because for Rahner, the 'apostolate' of the laity is based on being Christian and determined, not by a particular mission received from

---

[24] R. PELLLITERO, "Congar on the Laity" in J.A. DINOIA, o.p. (ed.), *The Thomist*, 65(2001), p.345. "According to Congar, in 1953 he was not trying to create a purely canonical definition, but rather a definition – better still, a description – that was anthropological."
[25] Ibid. p.328. See, T.I. MacDONALD, The Ecclesiology of Yves Congar: Foundational Themes, Milwaukee, 1981. See also, J. FAMEREE, L'ecclésiologie d'Yves Congar, avant Vatican II, histoire et église. analyse et reprise critique, Louvain, 1992.
[26] CONGAR, *Op. cit.* p.19ff. See, PELLLITERO, "Congar on the Laity", *Op. cit.* pp.343-344. Ramiro Pellitero a good commentator on Congar thinks that, "in the years immediately following *Jalons*, Congar used the insights of Karl Rahner to define the layperson as a Christian who embraces the conditions of his natural insertion in the world. Congar was attracted to this formula because it helped him to understand the lay condition in a way that was positive rather than negative, by means of an "internal characterisation" intrinsic to the same lay condition: the force of the temporal commitment."
[27] PELLLITERO, *Op. cit.* p.339.
[28] Y. M-J, CONGAR, Jalons pour une théologie du laïcat, (Unam Sanctam 23), Paris, 1953.

above, but rather by their existence in the world: "the plan of his Christian influence is the same as that of his relations in the world," from this Rahner deduced that, *"participating in the hierarchical apostolate...is to cease being a layperson."*[29] Yet we realize that the entire question recoils and turns around again,

The contemporary conversation shows the complicated nature of 'the theology of the Laity' then and today, years after Vatican II.

And 50-years after Vatican II counting – with the controversial synods: Amazon and German synodal path – no doubt that the question of the "apostolate of the laity" in light of the postmodern cultural developments and idiosyncrasies will no doubt put the Church and her teaching in a real quagmire. Be that as it may, the gospel of Jesus Christ and truly so must and should have priority of place - without distortion and misinterpretation to suit our "mere human selfish interests." *In spite of the fact that the Sabbath is meant for man and not man for the Sabbath* as some Critics will argue otherwise. As Cardinal Gerhard Müller succinctly and rightly so argued: 'True Reform of the Church Is About Her Renewal in Christ.'[30]

---

[29] K. RAHNER, "L'apostolat des laïcs," *Op. cit.* pp.15-22. *Italics mine.*
[30]Cf. https://catholiccitizens.org/views/87882/cardinal-gerhard-muller-true-reform-of-the-church-is-about-her-renewal-in-christ-2/ consulted on 21/01/2020.

3.2 Some Apostolic Fathers and 'the Laity-Question' - In the light of today's Controversial New Role of the Laity in the Church vis-à-vis the Amazon Synod and the German Synodal Path

The demised eminent Theologian-Scholar and one of the *groundwork-layers* of the *Lumen Gentium* of the Vatican II council - Monsignor Gerard Philips of Leuven Belgium succinct argument on the Laity maybe summarized as follows, that "every member of the *new community* – the Church, sanctified by the faith and by baptism, can be called 'Lay'. But from the very beginning this new community has been structured. It is in the light of this structuring that one finds the different orders and distinctions."[31] This fact became very glaring in some of the *Fathers of the Church* – briefly elucidated below:

(A) Clement of Rome is said to be the first Christian writer to use the word, '*laikos*'[32] – to designate the "laity." In a letter he wrote to the church in Corinth written about A.D 95, Clement, the presiding presbyter or proto-bishop of the Greek-speaking church in Rome, makes brief reference to the participants in the liturgy with the assertion: '…the Layman (*ho laikos anthropos*) is bound by the Lay (*laikos*) ordinances.'[33] Thus, in assigning the 'Layman' a liturgical role along with but subordinate to that of the presbyters and that of the

[31] PHILIPS, *Op. cit.* p.9. See, G. PHILIPS, "Wereldkongres van het lekenapostolaat," in *Ignis*, (1957) nr.11, pp.1-3.
[32] W. KASPER, et. al. *Lexikon für theologie und kirche*, (Sechster band), Freiburg, Basel, Rom, Wien, 1997.p.587. "Der Begriff λαικός kommt christlich erstmal in 1Clem. 40,5."
[33] ST CLEMENT OF ROME, Epis. to the Corinthians, 40, no.5 in F. X. FUNK, Patres Apostolici, Tubingen, 1909, Vol. I, p.151, L. KLEIST (trans), s.j. Ancient Christian Writers: The Epistles of St Clement of Rome and St Ignatius of Antioch, Westminster, London, 1949, p.34.

deacons, Clement is at once reflecting general Greek usage of the word 'Lay' and turning it in a specifically Christian direction. It is worth noting, that up till now this Greek term was used as an adjective to distinguish ordinary *mass of people* from their leaders.

However, when this letter of Clement was translated into Latin (about half a century later) the translator preserved something of the older pagan Greek feeling about the impropriety of applying *laikos* to persons; for, though he wrote in Latin *Lay ordinances* (*laicis praeceptis*), he preferred for 'the *Lay*man' the socially tinctured phrase *plebeius homo*.[34] However *plebian* or humble the role of the Layman, he was nevertheless from the beginning a participant in liturgical praise of the Creator and Redeemer of all human persons and not a merely spectator of the cultic mysteries.[35]

(B) St Ignatius, Bishops of Antioch (c.35-110A.D): In his letter addressed to the seven churches, he stressed the monarchical and the hierarchical structure of the local churches.[36] The implication was that churches were built on the distinction of orders, a distinction between the Laity and the Hierarchy – the *Laicus* as against the *Clericus*, whereby the idea of the former is equivalent 'to one who is not familiar with the inner affairs of the Church as such,' and so should be subservient to the hierarchy.

Ignatius teaches that all Lay activities should be exercised under the authority of the bishop. As he argues, "You should all follow the bishops as Jesus Christ did follow the Father. Nobody must do anything that has to do with the Church without the bishop's approval.

---

[34] POTTERIE, *Op. cit.* p.849.
[35] WILLIAMS, *Op. cit.* p.30.
[36] BIHLMEYER-H. TUCHLE, *Kirchengeschichte*, Paderborn, Vol. 1, *Christian Antiquity*, V.E. MILLS (trans), O.F.M., Maryland, 1958, pp.172-173.

Without the bishop's supervision, no baptism or agapes are permitted. On the other hand, whatever he approves pleases God as well. In that way everything you do will be on the safe side and valid. But he who acts without the bishop's knowledge is in the devil's service."[37]

(C) St Justin, the Martyr (c.100-165 A.D): Justin, the Martyr, in describing the Eucharistic supper and the active part, which the faithful[38] take therein, reinstated the principle of the priesthood of all believers. As he wrote, 'being inflamed by the word of his [Christ's] calling, we are the true high-priestly race of God.'[39] The implication of this was that, by his membership in the group, the Laity are persons 'consecrated,' though the *holy things* are especially entrusted to the clergy. But this kind of distinction is not to the liking of all.

It is worth noting that the Latin word *populus* is likewise opposed to the leaders in the celebrated Roman inscription S.P.O. R. – *senatus populusque romanus*, even though the senators should not be considered as if they did not belong to the general population. Similarly, this development is found in the use of the phrase 'the faithful' for the laity; the members of the clergy have nevertheless the same obligation to believe and as such they too are included to say among the faithful.[40]

(D) Irenaeus, Bishop of Lyon (c.130-200A.D): He speaks about the living magisterium in his work, *Adversus Haereses*, written about

[37] "The Letters to the Smyrnians," cap. VIII, I; the English translation taken from *Early Christian Fathers*, Vol. I, 115 of *The Library of Christian Classics*, edited and translated by C. C. RICHARDSON, London, 1952-1953.
[38] ST JUSTIN, *First Apology*, 67, 5; P.G., 6. See, H. KELLER & O. VON NELL BREUNING, *Das Recht der Laien in der Kirche,* Heidelberg, 1950, p.23. John Paul II capitalised upon this term, which we shall see more in chapter 3, in his text, *Christifideles Laici* (1989).
[39] *Ibid.* p.116.
[40] *Loc. cit.*

180-190A.D and existing in Latin translation made about 300 A.D.[41] Since the hierarchy in the person of the bishops are the custodians of the faith, and right interpreters of the doctrines, all faithful should *ipso facto* submit to their authorities in the teaching activities.[42] In the light of this type of theology, the authority of the hierarchy is outstanding,[43] and the laity are like pupils obeying their teacher command. The mission of the laity is as it where beclouded here in the bishops and hierarchy.

(E) Quintus Septimus Florens Tertullianus (c.160-220A.D): Tertullian stresses the priestly character of baptismal unction. For him, this qualifies the recipient to baptise in his turn, 'what is equally received can be equally given.'[44] At the same time, for the sake of order, he argues, before joining the Montanists, that what is lawful may not be expedient and the Laymen only should perform the sacrament and only in the absence of a Cleric; that Laywomen should never presume to baptise in any circumstance. But when he joined the Montanist camp he rejected this kind of distinction, between the clergy and the Laity.[45] Instead, he queried that, 'we Laymen, are not we also priests?'[46] It was in the charismatics and the 'illuminated' and not in the established authority that he recognised the spiritual power.

[41] K. BIHLMEYER-H.TUCHLE, *Op. cit.* pp.180-181.

[42] *Adversus Haereses*, lib. V. Praefatio, in *Patrologiae Cursus Completus* of J-P MIGNE, *Patrologiae Graecae,* t. 7, col. 1119-1120: "Apostoli vero tradiderunt, a quibus Ecclesia accipiens, per universum mundum sola benecustodians, tradidit filiis suis ...neophytorum quoque sensum confirmare, ut stabilem custodiant fidem, ut nullo modo transvertantur ab his, qui male docere eos, et abducere a veritate conantur."

[43] G. BARDY, *La théologie de l'eglise de saint Clément de Rome a saint Irénée*, (Coll. Unam Sanctam, n.13), Paris, 1945, pp.39-51.

[44] TERTULLIAN, *De Baptismo*, 7, in REIFFERSCHEID (ed.), CSEL XX, 206.

[45] See, A. FAIVRE, *Les laïcs aux origines de l'Eglise*, Paris, 1984. He attests that an "institutional barriers"(*une barrière institutionnelle*) was gradually erected, separating the clergy from the laity and eventually causing lay people to cease performing certain activities in the Church and in its official mission.

[46] TERTULLIAN, *Exhortatio ad castitatem*, 7, P.L., 2, p.922. "Nonne et laici sacerdotes sunt?" Note that while still being a Catholic, Tertullian considered this pretension as exorbitant.

Be that as it may, several studies published in the middle 1980s had shown that the terminology *kleros-laikos* was developed only in the third century. The term "laikos" was not even used by the early church fathers, apart from a brief reference in Clement of Rome's *Letter to the Corinthians*. The early Church directed its interest, instead, to the unity that existed among the members of the people of God. From approximately the time of Tertullian, however, the clergy began to be distinguished from Laity, and emphasis was placed more on the differentiation of functions in the Church than on unity.

The "institutional barriers" (*une barrière institutionnelle*) was gradually erected, separating the clergy from the laity and eventually causing lay people to cease performing certain activities in the Church and in its official mission.

Furthermore, in a recorded discussion on the 19th February 2001 (this writer – then, as a doctoral study on the *Vatican II and the Laity)* - this writer and Professor Dr. Mathijs Lamberigts, the then Dean of the faculty of Theology – himself an outstanding Church historian of the Catholic University Leuven Belgium (Flemish); the Dean - a historian of Vatican II, argued that 'Laicus' as one who is not familiar with the inner affairs of the Church was actually a Middle Age idea which in recent times is fast fading away.[47] Part of the reason is the fact of lack of vocation to the Priesthood, especially in Europe; such that the Laity are now being deployed more, in the inner Church's apostolate, unlike before Vatican II Council.

[47] Cf, M. LAMBERIGTS, "The 'Vota antepraeparatoria' of the Faculties of Theology of Louvain and Louvanium (Zaire)," in M. LAMBERIGTS & C. SOETENS (eds.), *A la veille du concile Vatican II. vota et réactions en Europe et dans le catholicisme oriental (Instrumenta Theologiae)*, Leuven, 1992.

(F) Thascius Caecilius Cyrianus (c.200-258A.D): He is of the opinion that the bishop should be chosen in the presence of the Laity who have most fully known the life of each one of several possible choices, and have looked into the doings of each one as regards his habitual conducts.[48] In fact, he insists that, just as the Laity has the power of recognition, they have also the power of withdrawing from the jurisdiction of an unworthy Cleric.[49]

(G) Gregory of Nazianzus (c.276-374 A.D): One of the outstanding things about Gregory, apart from taking theology to the 'bazaars and marketplaces'[50] among the Laity, was also his emphatic linking of spirituality to concrete social action. At a time when the very rich and very poor Laity were united in their services to the Church, he had advised the rich Laity, 'we must share our wealth with Christ, so that it may be sanctified, and shared with the poor.'[51]

(H) Augustinus (c.354-430AD): Augustine emphasised the universality of the evangelical mission for all the baptised, though, recognising grades of ministry in the Church; here he draws a basic distinction between the Laity and 'Ministers,' and between 'Ministers and the People.'[52]

He exhorted the Laity who he addressed as part of the body of Christ, to participate in the mission of Christ. He reiterated that the "Church, the Body of Christ spread throughout the whole world, preaches Christ. Therefore, Christ preaches Christ, the Body preaches its Head,

---

[48] CYPRIANUS, *Epistola*, 67.5. In *Epistola* 10.8, He speaks of Cornelius of Rome as made bishop by the judgment of God and Christ, by the testimony of the clerics, and by the vote (*suffragio*) of both the priests and the *plebs*.

[49] *Ibid.* 67.3.

[50] GREGORY OF NAZIANZUS, Sermon concerning the Deity of the Son: PG 46,557.

[51] GREGORY OF NAZIANZUS, *De Pauperum Amore* 18(*PG* 35,880).

[52] J. T. LIENHARD, "Ministry," in A.D. FITZGERALD, OSA, (ed) et. alii. *Augustine through the Ages. An Encyclopedia,* Michigan/Cambridge, 1999, p.568.

and the Head guards the Body. And therefore, the world hates us, as we have heard from the Lord Himself. For He did not say this to a few Apostles, that the world should hate them, but He said this to His whole Body, to all His members."[53]

However, one should note that Augustine is mindful of the fact that the Laity exercised the teaching apostolate according to their own way, which is different from that of the hierarchy.[54] By so doing, Augustine recognized different grades of ministry in the hierarchy and steps or degrees that led to it. He clearly knows the orders of acolyte, lector, sub-deacon, deacon, priest, and bishop. Whether he also knew the orders of exorcists and porter is uncertain.[55]

But as far as the Laity were concerned, Augustine notes that the Laity have their own special mission in the entire mission of the 'body of Christ' – that of reaching non-believers, since the Laity are sent by their bishops for their own tasks.

Whereas, the Laity have the mission of taking the message to those who are not present at the Christian assemblies; however, they should keep a close union with their bishop, for bishops are the only authentic teachers of the Church and the Laity are representing bishops. Thus, there is a dependence on the magisterium of the Church. Accordingly, for Augustine, the lay apostolate is essentially a participation of the Laity in the works of Christ, the King, Priest and Teacher, and it has to be exercised with and under bishops.

---

[53] "...Quoniam Christum ipse praedicat Christus, hoc est corpus Christi toto orbe diffusum, [...]. Praedicat ergo Christus, preadicat corpus caput suum, et tuetur caput corpus suum. Et ideo nos mundus odit, sicut ab ipso Domino audivimus (Joan. 15, 18-21). Non enim Apostolis hoc dicebat, quod odisset eos mundus; [...] sed dixit universo corpori suo, dixit omnibus membris suis" (Sermo 354, 1, in PL, tom, 39, col. 1563; the translation is taken from E.J, HUGHES, *The Participation of the Faithful in the Royal and Prophetic Mission of the Christ according to Saint Augustine*, Mundelein, 1956, p.51).

[54] ST. AUGUSTINE, *In Jo. Ev. Tractatus*, LI, 13, in PL, t.35, col.1768-1789.

[55] J. T. LIENHARD, *Loc. cit.*

From the epoch of the Middle Ages, the Church has started to distinguish between three states: the Lay, Clerical and Monastic. The state of the Lay was not so much a fact of definition as of something immediately given as a basis: the condition of Christians who were working out their salvation in the everyday life of the world. The clerical condition was seen in terms of service at the altar and the *religious* (Monks etc) role was seen as *service* to the Christian people - the Laity.

It is worth noting that, even the *monastic condition* in that epoch was not seen or defined by service of sacred things, not even by service of the altar – since this was clearly reserved for the *Klerus.* The first Monks in the Eastern Church had hardly any 'liturgical' life as such. The liturgy was by definition a public service, and therefore the business of Clerics, and in some Western monasteries the part of the monastic church used by the Laity was put in charge of Clerics who were not Monks.[56] At this time, professed religious who had charge of the manual labour in the monasteries were called *laici* in opposition to the *choir monks*. Hence, their state was sacred but their work was profane.[57] In this regard, there was a historical case of St Jerome, a monk, who did not wish to be a priest, and after he had been ordained he had his brother Paulinian *priested* to take care of the services of the monastery.

[56] E. DEKKER, "Les anciens moines cultivaient-ils la liturgie?" in *Vom Christl. Mysterium. Gesam. Arbeitem z. Gedachtnis* von O. Casel, Dusserldorf, 1951, pp.97-114..
[57] D.DU CANGE, *Glossarium mediae et infimae latinitatis*, s.v. *Laicus*. Tome V, Niort, 1885, p.15.

With time, these triple division: Laity, Clerics and Monks became assimilated or subsumed into: Clerics to Monks and Monks to Clerics – hence a double division into *men of religion* and *men of the world* was the end result. In sum, two things emerged: Lay position is presented as a concession, and its general tendency was to deny that the Laity, concerned in temporal affairs, have nothing to do in the sphere of sacred things.[58]

That the laity had no hand in the "Sacred things" by broader definition - is historically rebuffed by the fact that the laity in the form of the Kings (Emperors) times called for or convocated some so-called *Christian Councils* in the history of the Church. That most of these Councils were convoked/chaired by the laity in the form of Emperors is a historical fact.[59]

It is worth noting here that from the period of Nicea Council (325 AD), through the Vatican I till Vatican II (1962 – 1965 AD) are in total: *twenty-one councils*: namely - Nicea (325 AD), Constantinople (381 AD), Ephesus (431AD), Chalcedon (451 AD), Constantinople II (553 AD), Constantinople III (680-681AD), Nicea II (787 AD), Constantinople VI (869-870 AD), Lateran I (1123 AD), Lateran III (1179 AD), Lateran IV (1215 AD), Lyon I (1245 AD), Lyon II (1274 AD), Vienne (1312 AD), Basel (1437 AD - disputed?), Ferrara-Florence (1437-1439 AD), Lateran V (1512-1517 AD), Trent (1543-1563 AD), Vatican I (1869-1870 AD), Vatican II (1962 – 1965 AD).[60]

---

[58] CONGAR, *Op. cit.* p.12.

[59] Cf. DANIEL-ROPS, *The Second Vatican Council. The Story behind the Ecumenical Council of Pope John XIII,* A. GUINAN (trans.) New York, 1962,

[60] H. DANIEL-ROPS, *The Second Vatican Council.* p.28.

However, it is disputed by Church historians as to whether all these councils actually took place.[61]

Be that as it may, that some of these Christian Councils mentioned above where convoked and times chaired by the Laity is a historical fact. But the fact remains in the light of today´s development in *defining* new roles for the laity in the Church via the Synods: Amazon – German Synod Path - how do we put these historical facts in perspective with the new role that some laity are "demonstrating for" - advocating for or aspiring for in the Church today? How does one understand or view this *defining moment* in the light of the Amazon synod or the German synod path effort of defining "new role for the laity in the Church?"

[61] H. DANIEL-ROPS, *Loc. cit.*

Chapter Four

4. The Laity as the *people of God*: Yves Marie-Joseph Congar (OP) vis-a-vis the Vatican II´s nuance in relation to the *viri probati*[62] concept of *Amazon Synod* vis-à-vis the *German Synod Path*

4.1 Preamble

It is plausible to say that the Laity are: 'Christians in the full sense of the word' *ipso facto* are members of the Church, *the People of God.*[63]

Thus, from an integral-ecclesiological[64] point of view every Christian, whether belonging to the hierarchy or a monk or a simple believer so to say, is basically a baptized person; all the baptized are bound together in a common obedience to the same Lord and Saviour, Jesus Christ, which admits of no dichotomy; since all, as members of the λάος, the people of God – the Laity.

4.2 Yves Marie-Joseph Congar

A tribute is worth giving to Yves Marie-Joseph Congar (OP) who developed this *integral ecclesiology* earlier on, in his *Unam Sanctam* series[i] before even the Vatican II Council (1962 – 1965). It is worth noting that Yves Congar began his theological journey in the 1930s,

62 See: *Who are viri probati* in *www.romereports.com*, consulted on 18/01/2020.
63 Cf, K. RAINIER, "De zonde in de Kerk", in G. BARAÚNA (ed.), *De Kerk van Vaticanum II. Commentaren op de Concilieconstitutie over de Kerk,* vol. I, Bilthoven, 1966, p. 439.
64 The Chapter II of *Lumen Gentium*, Dogmatic Constitution on the Church is titled: "The People of God" – here this integral-ecclesiology is developed on and before the Chapters on the Hierarchy and the Laity. See Chapter II of this project for details.

years that witnessed the ascendancy of the de-Christianization that had been progressing in Central Europe since the end of the nineteenth century. As a theologian and a man of the Church, Congar drew upon his Thomistic education, formed in the theological school of *Le Saulchoir,* in his search for answers to the pastoral challenges of the time. During these years, Congar figured among the driving forces in the re-evaluation of the role of the laity, within the context of the French Catholic Action movements. In these same years, he was responsible for introducing into France the great ecclesiology of Tubingen, centered in the works of Johann Adam Möhler, in which the Church appears as a living organism extending herself through history under the impetus of the Holy Spirit. Theology and Pastoral preoccupations intersected in the thought of the celebrated Dominican, enriching one another and offering fruits that translated into intellectual enterprises, publications, and in the "ecumenical vocation" of Congar.

Yves Marie-Joseph Congar (OP), in his encounters with the laity (and within the context of the Catholic Action movement), spoke of the personal spiritual life and the Christian transformation of society. In order to provide a foundation for the ecclesial vision of the laity, he turned to the theology of the Mystical Body, *then at the height of its popularity, and to the vision of the common priesthood of the faithful.* We may identify the following phases in Congar's thinking about the figure of the *layperson and his mission*:

(1) a primary stage marked by the theology of the Mystical Body during the 1930s and 1940s.

(2) his book *Jalons pour une théologie du laïcat* (1953), which remains Congar's best-known approach to the topic.

(3) a stage which may be considered his most glorious, coinciding with the years of the Second Vatican Council in the 1960s.

(4) a period, during the years immediately following the council – the reconsideration of his positions, with regard to the so-called "theology of ministries."

(5) A final stage, which we could call a period of simplification and return to the core of his thought, during the 1980s. The hermeneutical thesis of Congar may be summed up as follows: '*thought about the person and the responsibility of lay Christians may be understood in light of a double source: his vision of the relation between the Church and the World and his deepening sense of the threefold structure of the Church (ordained ministers, laity, and religious).*'

In sum, following an historical study of the sources, Congar concludes by saying that the Laity are the "Christians who sanctify themselves in the life of this *saeculum.* In order words, the Laity are called to the same end as the clergy and religious, but they achieve this end "without sparing themselves the commitment to the movement of this world, in the realities of the first creation, in the periods, stages and movements of history. Even more precisely, he adds that the Laity are called to do "the work of God in this world," emphasizing "to the same degree which it ought to be carried out in and by the work of the world." *Essentially, the layperson values things "in themselves."* Congar does not stop here, but goes a step further. He writes that the layperson must be "the one for whom, in the same work which God has entrusted to him, the substance of things in themselves exists and is interesting." For the cleric, and even more for the religious, explains Congar, worldly things are of interest not so much in or for themselves, or because of the demands of their nature, as for their reference to God, for their significance.

In Sum, for the thirty years before the council was called, Congar was one of the key figures in the theological renewal of Catholicism in the twentieth century. Besides hundreds of scholarly articles, Congar wrote major works on ecumenism, on reform, and *on the laity* that did as much as anyone else's works to help Catholics recover long-neglected traditions and to derive from them inspiration for a more creative engagement with their own world. After labouring for decades under Roman suspicion, Congar was to see much of his vision of the church vindicated by Vatican II Coucnil.

4.3 Vatican II nuance - "the Laity" in relation to the *viri probati (Tested Married men)*

We begin here with *Lumen Genium* since this document of the Vatican II apart from being the "oldest and first formulated document of the Council" - it forms equally the nexus to other documents of the Council in the laity-question vis-à-vis issues.

Essentially in Lumen Gentium, *the mystery of the Church*[65] is first expressed in the first chapter, followed by the mystery of Christian life, in the context of the People of God.[66] According to Willems, the *notion of mystery* is an ambiguous term that quickly loses its dynamism when incorrectly interpreted. He expresses his concern as follows: "When the use of the word 'mystery' is understood as an

---

[65] See also this commentator; A. WILLEMS, "Het mysterie als ideologie. De bisschoppensynode over het kerkbegrip" In *Tijdschrift voor Theologie*, 26 [1986] 164.

[66] KOBLER, "The New Ecclesial Hermeneutics", in *Vatican II and Phenomenology. Reflections on the Life-World of the Church,* p.118."

objectivized (sic), nearly physical presence, there is a *per-versio,* a theological perversion with negative results for the faith and the Church."

This "integral ecclesiology"[67] clearly precedes the discussion of the Hierarchy and the specific Lay ministries.[68] The priority given to the understanding of Church as the People of God is according to Gehard Philips concentrated in the idea of *communion:*[69] "After a long period of individualism the spirit of ecumenism, which had long been treated with reserve, if not with downright suspicion, gained full rights of citizenship in the Roman Catholic Church".[70] With this shifting of ground in ecclesiology "Vatican II moved away from the thinking of Pius IX who gave credence to Vatican I – with the task of ratifying this conception of the Church as a society in which authority "descends" from the top, and communion among the members is mediated through the dependence of all on the authority of the pope alone. The result was an ecclesiology not unknown before, but never sanctioned either in its structure or in the central place given to it in the Christian economy. But with Vatican II's *Lumen gentium,*

[67] Congar had before the 'official Council' referred to this as the 'integral-ecclesiology' and had developed this scheme within his text prior to the documents of Vatican II. Cf. *Jalons pour une theologie du laïcat,* Paris, 1953, pp.81-84. This had influenced the document in its theological formulation in this regard.

[68] Loc. cit.

[69] Willems reiterates that the idea of the Church as communio (as concrete expression of the Church as mystery) is used as a fortress behind which the themes that many consider urgent, such as the relationship of local churches to Rome and episcopal collegiality must be contained; *Op. cit.* p.166, pp.169-170.

[70] G. PHILIPS, "History of the Constitution," in H. VORGRIMLER, *Commentary on the Documents of Vatican II. Dogmatic Constitution on the Church,* Vol.1, K. SMYTH, (trans.), New York, 1966, p.105. 'It is worthy of note, that after the declaration of the Holy Office in 1949 and erection of a Secretariat for the promoting of the unity of Christians, by John XXIII, this gave strong impulse to the effort to make contact with non-Catholic Christians.'
See also, A. THIJS en J. VERSTRAETEN, "De leek op het snijpunt van geloof en wereld" in: *Collationes. Vlaams Tijdschrift voor Theologie en Pastoraal,* 17(1987), pp.139-151. "Vanuit haar verbondenheid met Christus is de kerkgemeenschap als 'volk Gods' bovendien geroepen om een teken van eenheid te zijn....Deze *communio* mag niet worden opgevat als een dorre uniformiteit, omdat zij een *levende* eenheid in *verscheidenheid* is." *Ibid.* p.142.

ecclesiology thus reached levels that were new in relation to the entire Christian tradition."[71]

Reflecting on this historical issue, Willems, opines that 'the one-sided[72] jettison of the view of Church as *People of God* was related to the council that, in viewing the Church as the *People of God*, expressly stepped back from a fundamentally clerical view of the Church, electing instead a salvation historical approach. A changed hermeneutic context brought to light still another aspect of the expression *People of God* that received little attention during the council: the political dimension, oriented pragmatically toward a process of change in the life of the Laity in the world.[73] It is worthy of note, that the council could not foresee this since it only started to affect theology only in the 1970s.'[74]

However, it is worth noting as Kobler succinctly acknowledged, that the origin of the concept, '*people of God'* was introduced to American readers in 1937 even ahead of the Vatican II Council, but was only adopted in Vatican II and that this concept goes back to the earlier work of Dom Anscar Vonier, O.S.B., an eminently respected writer on things spiritual and theological. He argued that at the Council, "the bishops were quite faithful to Vonier's original purpose for this imagery when they turned to reflect on the "flesh and blood" dimensions of the Church: that is - the meaning for them of concrete humanity's ordering to God. This "sense" of their religious life-world began to take the form of three ecclesiocentric "horizons" correlating Catholics, Christians, and all the unbaptized. Paul VI, as one may

[71] ALBERIGO, *Op. cit.* pp.14-15.
[72] Regarding the shifted accent on the Church as People of God see details in the article by J-M, TILLARD, "Final Report of the Last Synod", *Concilium*, 188 [1986] 6, 67-68.
[73] WILLEMS, "Het mysterie als ideologie. De bisschoppensynode over het kerkbegrip," p.164.
[74] ALBERIGO, *Op. cit.* 2.""

recall, used a somewhat comparable imagery in *Ecclesiam Suam*. Now, however, the bishops' principle of spiritual discernment (or eidetic analysis) is quite different. Although verbalized in an extrinsic way as God's universal call to salvation."[75]

The Dogmatic Constitution, *Lumen gentium* maybe said to have laid the foundation but essentially not the details of the Laity theology - *Apostolicam actuositatem* did.[76] According to Cardinal Lorscheider a delegate at the Council, the reason for this is that, "There was a fear in some quarters that the image of the 'people of God' in *Lumen Gentium* had been misunderstood and had given rise to a view of the Church that was 'sociological' rather than 'theological', creating the danger of a degeneration into a merely 'democratic view' of the Church.

Perhaps this so called "democratic view" of the Church is what we are seeing in a mild way being expressed in the two synods (*Amazon synod* and *German synodal path*) under discussion in this project.

Be that as it may - what we see in the document *(Lumen gentium*) mentioned above by the theologians at the Council was the general focus of the document on the nature and inner structure of the Church. According to them this has to do with the *essence* of the Church[77] - with particular reference to 'the mission of proclaiming and establishing among all peoples the kingdom of Christ and of God.'[78] While they tried to establish the base for this mission, they failed to

[75] KOBLER, "The New Ecclesial Hermeneutics," *Loc. cit.,*
[76] Loc. cit.
[77] LOBO, *Op. cit.* p.2.
[78] *L.G.* n. 5. "Missionem accipit Regnum Christi et Dei annuntiandi et in omnibus gentibus instaurandi, huiusque Regni in terris germen et initium constituit."

present the full implication of this mission to the world according to a critic.[79] Note that this became a later engagement of the Synod of Bishops on the vocation and mission of the laity (1987) with its dossier being the product of *Christifideles laici* of John Paul II.

Be as it may, the 'theology of the laity' in the document' mentioned, [80] grew naturally as it where from the doctrine of the Church as the body of Christ and into the notion of people of God. Of course, this latter concept as deployed by the theologians at the council does not refer to the faithful as a group in contrast to the hierarchy, but to the Church in its totality including all its members without regard to their ministry or state.[81] *Integral ecclesiology* is instead the hermeneutical key to the understanding of the role of the people of God at least in chapter 2 of *Lumen gentium*. In the chapters that followed - the situation becomes more complex. Chapter 3 sees the activities of the clergy as materially derived from the Church and in chapter 4 of the same *Lumen gentium* - those of the laity, as it where are said to derive from the nature of the world in which they are engaged, thus, it "pertains to them in a special way so to illuminate and order all temporal things with which they are so closely associated that these may be effected and grow according to Christ and may be to the glory of the Creator and Redeemer."[82]

In the midst of this seemingly dichotomy, the document tried to create a nexus between the laity and the clergy by way of using the analogy

---

[79] LOBO, *Op. cit.* p.3. Note that this became a later engagement of the Synod of Bishops on the vocation and mission of the laity (1987) with its dossier being the product of *Christifideles laici* of John Paul II.

[80] A. HASTINGS, A Concise Guide to the Documents of the Vatican II, Vol. 1, London, 1968, p.49.

[81] A. GRILLMEIER, "Kommentar zur Lumen Gentium" in Lexikon für Theologie und Kirche, Zweite, völlig neu bearbeitete Auflage. Das Zweite Vatikanische Konzil. Dokumente und Kommentare, Teil.1, Freiburg, 1966, p.176.

[82] *L. G. n. 5.* "Ad illos ergo peculiari modo spectat res temporales omnes, quibus arete coniunguntur, ita illuminare et ordinare, ut secundum Christum iugiter fiant et crescant et sint in laudem Creatoris et Redemptoris."

of the body.[83] What unites the clergy and laity in brotherhood is the common call to perfection, whereas, functionally, both are different. "In the Church not, everyone marches along the same path, yet all are called to sanctity and have obtained an equal privilege of faith through the justice of God."[84]

A further link is made here between the hierarchy at mission and the Laity. 'In the past the Lay apostolate was sometimes defined as the co-operation of the laity in the apostolate of the hierarchy.'[85] This way of definition was not a good one[86] - because of the deficiency of this expression, 'participation in the apostolate of the hierarchy' at the World Laity Congress, the word, 'corroboration' was introduced, but rejected participants. It was then, that Cardinal Suenens of Belgium, the relator at the Council introduced the word, 'co-responsibility,' which participants admitted and cherished most.

Since, the hierarchy has a function proper to them and so do the laity. The Lay apostolate comes primarily, not from a special offer to do part of the hierarchy's job for it, but from the obligation of every baptized Christian to share actively in the mission of Christ.[87] Evidently many Laymen and women are called over and above this to be very important. But basically, *the lay apostolate is precisely that apostolate which is proper to Laity, which as Christians; they do not*

[83] *L. G.* n. 32. "Sicut enim in uno corpore multa membra habemus, omnia autem membra non eundem actum habent: ita multi unum corpus sumus in Christo, singuli autem alter alterius membra (Rom.12, 4-5)."
[84] *Loc. cit.* "Si igitur in Ecclesia non omnes eadem via incedunt, omnes tamen ad sanctitatem vocantur et coaequalem sortiti sunt fidem in iustitia Dei."
[85] Cf. See especially, G. PHILIPS, "The Laity and Catholic Action" in *The Role of the Laity in the Church, Op. cit*, p.112-131; especially the subtitle, "Participation or Collaboration" *Ibid.* p.119.
[86] GOLDIE, *Loc. cit.*
[87] *L. G.* n. 35. "Christus, Propheta magnus, qui et testimonio vitae et verbi virtute Regnum proclamavit Patris, usque ad plenam manifestationem gloriae suum munus propheticum adimplet, non solum per Hierarchiam, quae nomine et potestate Eius docet, sed etiam per laicos…."

share in the hierarchical ministry. It is worth noting here, that article 34 of *Lumen gentium* is in a way a repetition of article 10 to 11; and article 35 in part of article 12. Accordingly, this must have happened when the old chapter on 'the people of God and the Laity' was split into two, and the former sections dealing with the priestly and prophetical aspects of Christian living were carried to Chapter 2. [88]

Subsequently, the document stressed the Laity's most concrete and characteristic way of implementing this apostolate in concrete through marriage and family life as being of some special importance in this 'prophetic office.'[89]

At this juncture a kind of transition takes place in the document. Thus, this prophetic role of the Laity as stated above is now extended to a wider network: reordering the earth, human culture and society, by this way ensuring that the kingdom of Christ is advanced – "and the field of the world is better prepared for the seed of the divine word."[90]

In this task, the document solicits for a co-operation between the clergy and Laity,[91] even though its style remains rather 'hierarchical-oriented.'[92] Yet, it canvasses that the health of the Church depends upon mutual trust and sharing of responsibilities between hierarchy and Laity; yet, "each individual layman must be a witness before the world to the resurrection and life of the lord Jesus, and a sign of the

---

[89] *L. G.* n. 35. "Quo in munere magni apparet ille status vitae, qui speciali sacramento sanctificatur, scilicet vita matrimonialis et familiaris. Ibi exercitium et schola praeclara apostolatus laicorum habetur, ubi religio christiana totam vitae institutonem pervadit et in dies magis transformat."
[90] *L. G.* n 36. "Hoc modo simul ager mundi melius pro semine verbi divini paratur, et Ecclesia latius patent portae, quibus praeconium pacis in mundum introeat."
[91] *L. G.* n 37. "Ex hoc familiari commercio inter Laicos et pastores permulta bona Ecclesiae exspectanda sunt: ita enim in laicis roboratur propriae responsabilitatis sensus, fovetur alacritas, et facilius laicorum vires Pastorum operi associantur. Hi vero, laicorum experientia adiuti, tam in rebus spiritualibus quam in temporalibus, distinctius et aptius iudicare valent, ita ut tota Ecclesia, ab omnibus membris suis roborata, suam pro mundi vita missionem efficacius compleat."
[92] A. HASTING *(ed.), Op. cit.* p.51.

living God."[93] The general outlook of this chapter on the laity seems to be on the 'outward-looking side' of the Church.

The result of this is that this document seemed to have focused too much attention on the role of the Layman and woman in the Church and not enough on the role of the Christian in the world.[94] This fragmented rather than inclusive approach, this lack of theological synthesis, encouraged the Lay believer to experience the Council via this document as a 'liturgical activity limited to an isolated parish setting.'[95]

On the other hand, even when it talks about mission as *witness,* as in the text: "they are called by God that, being led by the spirit to the Gospel, they may contribute to the sanctification of the world, as from within like leaven, by fulfilling their own particular duties. Thus, especially by the witness of their life, resplendent in faith, hope, and charity they must manifest Christ to others. It pertains to them to illuminate and order all temporal things with which they are so closely associated that these may be effected and grow according to Christ and may be to the glory of the Creator and Redeemer."[96] In light of the on-going, the Laity must be the sacrament of the living God before the world. What the soul is in the body, let the Christians be in the world."[97]

---

[93]*L. G.* n. 38. "Unusquisque laicus debet esse coram saeculo testis resurrectionis et vitae Domini Iesu atque signum Dei vivi."
[94] GOLDIE, *Op. cit.* p.60.
[95] V.S. FINN, "Laity: Mission and Ministry" in L. RICHARD, O.M.I, (Ed.), et al. *Vatican II: The Unfinished Agenda. A Look to the Future*, New York / Mahwah, 1987, p.149.
[96] *L. G.* n. 31. "Ibi a Deo vocantur, ut suum proprium munus exercendo, spiritu evangelico ducti, fermenti instar ad mundi sanctificationem velut ab intra conferant, sicque praeprimis testimonio vitae suae, fide, spe et caritate fulgentes, Christum aliis manifestent. Ad illos ergo peculiari modo spectat res temporales omnes, quibus arcte coniunguntur, ita illuminare et ordinare, ut secundum Christum iugiter fiant et crescant et sint in laudem Creatoris et Redemptoris."
[97] *L.G.* n. 38. "Uno verbo, quod anima est in corpore, hoc sint in mundo christiani."

This would entail an existential presence and concrete involvement in the society of humankind - relations, the family life etc. In reality, this would actually pave the way for authentic realisation of the Church′s mission via the Laity in the world. And this is the 'specific difference' of the Laity.

From the above discussions so far, more so, as Congar argued that, '*Lumen gentium (and Gaudium et spes*) must be read in connection with the other conciliar texts, the *Decree on the Apostolate of the Laity* (which is also based on the constitution on the Church, *Lumen gentium*) they are on the same lines as the Catholic Action inaugurated by Pius XI. This involves no claim to power over society but endeavours to act in society, to undertake that kind of non-violent action which we call influence, the chief instrument of which is bearing witness.'[98]

It behooves to say that the Dogmatic constitution on the Church, *Lumen gentium* forms the hermeneutical base for a better reading and understanding of the basic text of *Apostolicam actuositatem*, the decree on the apostolate of the Laity (even a later document, *Gaudium et spes*).[99] For the reason that, "the Decree *Apostolicam actuositatem,* the first document that a council has ever dedicated entirely to the Laity, places itself necessarily and perfectly within the global design of the Council, as a specific development of the integral ecclesiology

[98] Y. CONGAR, "The Role of the Church in the Modern World" in H. VORGRIMLER, (eds.), et al. *Commentary on the Documents of Vatican II. The Pastoral Constitution on the Church in the Modern World,* Vol. V, New York, 1969, p.214.

[99] *Loc. cit.* "*Lumen Gentium* (and *Gaudium et Spes)* must be read in connection with the other conciliar texts, the *Decree on the Apostolate of the Laity* (itself based on the constitution on the Church). They are on the same lines as the Catholic Action inaugurated by Pius XI. This involves no claim to power over society but endeavours to act in society, to undertake that kind of non-violent action which we call influence, the chief instrument of which is bearing witness."

of the Dogmatic Constitution *Lumen gentium* and of the Pastoral Constitution *Gaudium et spes*."[100]

It is precisely the fact that the laity has not been called for a special office or religious state, and that it is free from those special and lasting commitments connected with holy orders and the religious profession, which gives them those special opportunities and tasks which they would not have as clerics or as religious, although these tasks are of the greatest importance for the Church and the world, to mention only the field of political engagement, for example."

In this light of this explanation, it is worth understanding that the decree is addressed especially to those 'Laymen and women' who live "in the midst of the world and of secular transactions."[101] *In the opinion of this writer this would not mean isolating the 'laity' in participating in the 'ad intra' mission of the Church – of course Sancrosanctum concilium, the Constitution on the Sacred Liturgy (n.19) talks about this aspect of participation in the mission of the Church*). "Of course, this cannot be said to cover all those who are not clerics or religious."[102] However, the Church urgently needed the laity to help the bishops in their apostolate. It had to be written (the decree) because the Laity are the People of God. They are the Church – co-responsible with bishops, priests, and religious for Christ's mission on earth. This sense of *co-responsibility* is vital because of the widening gap between the modern world and the message of the gospel."

Be that as it may, it is worth noting that the term 'People of God' is, in any case, the core around which the Vatican II whole ecclesiology is

---

[100] JOHN PAUL II, "Faith of Laity must become life, culture, morality, mission" In *L'Osservatore Romano* (English edition), no.48 (914), 2 December 1985, p.13.
[101] R. PELLLITERO, "Congar on the Laity" in J.A. DINOIA, o.p. (ed.), *The Thomist*, 65(2001), pp.339-340. " Also, WORK, *Ibid*. p. 488.
[102] KLOSTERMANN, *Loc. cit.*,

structured. Consequently, the genus[103] of the term "Laity" comprises "all the faithful who by baptism are incorporated into Christ" and share in the priestly, prophetic and kingly office of Christ. On this level, everything is addressed equally to all: laity, religious and clergy. Thus, "in Christ and in the Church, there is then no inequality arising from race or nationality, social condition or sex, for "there is neither Jew nor Greek; there is neither slave nor freeman; there is neither male nor female. For you all are one in Christ Jesus."[104]

However, it is worth noting that the "laity" are equally part of the *arms of the Church* in terms of the *specific definition* - this leads to the search for a difference (specific) which actually was nuanced in the decree on the apostolate of the laity – *Apostolicam Actuositatem* – the decree on the apostolate of the laity. Suffice it to say that, *Lumen gentium* recognizes that not all members of the Church have the same gifts or particular mission and that, therefore, there will be a "wonderful diversity in the Church." *Lumen gentium* being the "heart" of the Vatican II document – invariably *Apostolicam Actuositatem* takes it "source" from Lumen Gentium – the dogmatic document on the people of God. Accordingly, *Ministeria Quaedam*, the document issued by Paul VI in 1972, by which the discipline of first tonsure, minor orders and sub diaconate in the Latin Church is reformed - identifies the clergy as the reception of Holy Orders which occurs first at the conferral of the deaconate and then the public profession to observe the evangelical counsels of poverty, chastity and obedience –

---

[103] Note that the 'deference' of the genus is considered in Chapter II, precisely on the 'typological nature' of the laity, in *Apostolicam Actuositatem*, the decree on the apostolate of the laity.

[104] *L. G.* n.32. "...In Christo et in Ecclesia inaequalitas, spectata stripe vel natione, condicione sociali vel sexu, quia non est Iudaeus neque Graecus: non est servus neque liber: non est masculus neque femina. Omnes enim vos "unus" estis in Christos Iesu Gal.3: 28; Col.3: 11." cf. 'Ministeria Quaedam' AAS, 64(1972), 529-534. All English translations of the Documents of Vatican II in this research are taken from, N. P. TANNER, S.J., (ed.) *Decrees of the Ecumenical Councils, Vol. II (Trent to Vatican II)*, London, 1990.

here it is worth noting that “celibacy” is implicit. How would and where would one really “classify” the *viri probati in the light of the foregoing nuances and the classifications before now?*

Chapter Five

Evaluation and General Conclusion:

Amazon synod vis-à-vis *German synodal path*: from the binocular of an African Theologian

For the first time in the entire history of the Catholic Church - there are "two-living-clearly-elected-Popes": One in retirement - the German and "world-best-theologian-alive" Pope Benedict XV1 and the incumbent - Pope Francis - Italian-born-Argentinian. While the former is a "diocesan priest" - the latter Pope Francis is a "Jesuit." It is paradoxical to say – that the Jesuits worthy of note are part of the so called "think-tanks" of the Church. – and often more "liberal arm" of the Catholic Church. This writer from experience had part of his theological study in katholieke Universiteit Leuven Belgium under some Jesuits. Pope Francis being a "Jesuit" is naturally "more liberal" in thought and ways of doing things. It´s a paradoxical statement! On these two Popes - the retired and incumbent "hang" this "hidden secret-divide" in the synods. In sum - it's a problem of "Loyalists." Although Pope Benedict is retired but still lives in the Vatican - he has still some and very faithful followers – *Augustiniarum* as against the so called *St Galen*.

The "second hidden issue behind this divide in the synods" is that Pope Benedict is against so called "Liberation Theology" - which he as Professor before he became a Pope was against because of the so called "Karl Marx philosophy undertone." On the other hand - the founders and real defenders of "liberation theology" in the Catholic

Church are mostly Jesuits from Latin America or evangelized in Latin American environ - India etc: for example - Leornardo Boff, Amarados (Indian Jesuit) and Gustavo Gutiérrez. "Liberation Theology" stresses that the "gospel of Christ is for the Emancipation of the poor in Latin America" and in poor countries - where mostly the Jesuit brought the faith too. On the contrary, most western theologians like Pope Benedict (Real name: Joseph Ratzinger") think otherwise.

Paradoxically "the so called Liberation theology" got its undertone from Johann Baptist Metz *"mysterium passionis"* theology: Metz a theologian and a Catholic Priest from Oberpfalz Bayern (confer: J. B. Metz, *Zur Begriff der neuen Politischen Theologie (1957 – 1967),* Mainz, 1997). Some of these liberation theologians from Latin America passed through him as students – it´s worth noting.

Paradoxically stated - on these two mentioned above issues among others lie the seemingly hidden divide and two main different voices in these Synods.

What we are watching play out in these "synods" - were longest time rooted, experimented, in the Universities of learning where these Synods are taking place. My experience as student in three of the best European Universities: KULeuven Belgium, LMU Munich, and Angelicum Rome - gave one such impression. I witnessed as a student "concelebrating" at mass in one of the University parishes where a "laywoman" - reads the gospel and preaches at mass. She was not "ordained" nor a deacon. This was as far back as 2001.

Again in a situation for example where a "Catholic Priest" from Ordination has "a lady – house-help" not a blood relation (although some are) and the Priest lives from the day of Ordination till retirement with such a lady and the people of God accept it in their parish-setting – what difference will it make - if the Priest is as well married? What of a situation where a Catholic Priest is already blessing “lesbians/homosexuals” with his own ritual in his church? There is also the so called problem of “cohabitation." And of those who are divorced etc. So, they so called “Synods” are just a way of raising “official theological questions, arguments – enquiry and perhaps suggestions to these sociological realities before our face in the Latin and Western world.

The onerous questions are: Where does and would the Church in Africa belong in these whole setups of the *synods (though synods are unique to particular church unique problem but still?)* and such thoughts – with her “excess priests?” Excess vocation? Imagine 4-priests in a parish in Africa - each living with their “wives” – the idea of “married priests”? The idea of needing foreign priests as “missionaries” abroad - will be reduced to minimum and a new “catholic morality” perhaps will be in place: how would African church with direct obedience and subservient to Rome see all these? Your guess is as good as mine!

The present crop of African theologians only studied “Western Theology” - we are only trying to interpret “the church” and her teachings to be meaningful to our people. Our people are not yet “strong” to digest the fast moving ships of Latin American Church with liberation theology and the Western European Church that is over 1000-years old. *Quid a casu?*

In sum, the outcome of these unique synods and their application in concrete – when and where will be anybody´s guess. But one thing is sure – their outcome will be very “critical for the future of the ministerial priesthood” and the universal Church in general and African church in particular – their echoes no doubt will reach that continent. Let’s keep watching and praying!

About the Book

Generally, Synods are good steps in bringing humans together - "Christians" in the Church to discussion on salient issue(s) affecting the Church. Since, dialoging is human – there is no harm in holding "Synods." However, in the light of the *title-issue* under discussion in this book - this book makes the case that the lay apostolate is precisely that apostolate which is proper to Laity, which as Christians, they do not share in the hierarchical ministry.

In the light of this - it is worth noting here, that article 34 of *Lumen gentium* is in a way a repetition of article 10 to 11; and article 35 in part of article 12. Accordingly, this must have happened when the old chapter on 'the people of God and the Laity' was split into two at the Vatican II Council, and the former sections dealing with the priestly and prophetical aspects of Christian living were carried to Chapter 2.

Be that as it may, these synods are very unique – the will no doubt raise dust and the echoes no doubt; and no doubt these echoes will reach beyond the borders of Europe into the African continent.

About the Author

Peter Chidi Okuma is a priest of the Catholic diocese of Orlu, Nigeria. He holds a Diploma with Distinction in Freelance and Feature Writing in Journalism from The London School of Journalism, United Kingdom. He also holds three Masters Degrees in Religious Studies, Education/Psychology, and Theology from the Catholic University of Leuven, Belgium, where he obtained a certified doctoral training in Theology in 2005, and proceeded to obtain a doctorate in Theology at the Ludwig Maximillian University Munich Germany and a second doctorate in Social Science at St. Thomas Aquinas University Rome (Angelicum). He has authored 16-national and International books and numerous articles. He currently resides and works in Germany.

Printed by Books on Demand GmbH, Norderstedt / Germany